B R E A ... ing

COMPULSIVE

OVEREATING

CHARISMA
HOUSE

LINDA MINTLE, PH.D.

BREAKING FREE FROM COMPULSIVE OVEREATING
by Linda S. Mintle, Ph.D.
Published by Charisma House
A part of Strang Communications Company
600 Rinehart Road
Lake Mary, Florida 32746
www.charismahouse.com

Cover design by Debbie Lewis
Interior design by David Bilby

Copyright © 2002 by Linda S. Mintle, Ph.D.
All rights reserved

Library of Congress Catalog Card Number:
2002108797

International Standard Book Number:
0-88419-898-7

02 03 04 05 06 — 8 7 6 5 4 3 2 1
Printed in the United States of America

Since Eve ate the apple, much depends on dinner.

—LORD BYRON

CONTENTS

"I try not to look in the mirror."

"I can't stop eating no matter what I do."

"I hate shopping for clothes."

"I think I've tried **every** *diet in America."*

"I CAN LOSE WEIGHT, BUT I CAN'T ***keep*** IT OFF."

"I don't look at myself below the neck."

"People just think I am lazy."

"I hate my body. It's gross."

"When I'm overweight I feel protected."

"I EAT WHEN I'M HAPPY, MAD, EXCITED, WHEN-EVER...*I just eat!*"

"I'm out of control but can't seem to stop!"

INTRODUCTION

CAN YOU RELATE?

Julie

Julie is frustrated with her weight. She has been steadily gaining for months and can't stop bingeing on candy. The more her weight goes up, the more depressed she becomes. Every night Julie promises herself that she'll be "good." Tomorrow she'll start a diet and get control of her eating. But tomorrow turns out like today—she eats compulsively.

It's hard for Julie to tell the difference between physical hunger and eating out of boredom or stress. She hates feeling this out of control and won't look at her body in the mirror.

Julie is a compulsive overeater who binges and "grazes" all day on food. She picks a little here, a little there, until she has grossly overeaten and gained weight. The compulsion to eat is emotionally based, but it is adding physical pounds to her 5 foot 2 inch frame. Julie reports she can't get control, vows daily to diet and fails.

Rita

"'Just go on a diet!' That's what people constantly tell me," Rita exclaims. "Like it's that easy to lose weight! If it was, don't you think I would have done it by now? Do people really think I enjoy carrying around this extra weight? I can hardly breathe when I walk. I'm always tired, and I can't ride bikes with my child. It's not fun. Yet, I can't seem to stop the compulsive eating. When I get really upset, I find myself binge-ing, especially on pizza and subs.

"I could write a book on dieting. I've tried Optifast, Slim Fast, Weight Watchers, the Atkins Diet—you name it, and I've done it. And I still weigh close to 250 pounds. Nothing seems to work. I just feel deprived when I diet."

Terry

Terry tells me, "I know my compulsive eating has something to do with being raped when I was twenty. When it happened, I was thin. This may sound crazy, but I feel like my weight protects me. When I'm overweight, men don't pay much attention to me, and I don't have to deal with them. Since I was date raped, I'm afraid to date. I guess I feel that staying big keeps men away. I know this weight is unhealthy. My joints hurt, and I feel so out of control, but I can't seem to stop. When I start to lose weight, I feel really anxious, almost panicked. It's too scary."

James

"I know my eating isn't healthy," says James. "I binge a lot, almost daily. I'm really shy and unsure of myself around women. Whenever I have to go to something social, I feel really anxious. I can control my eating in front of people, but when I'm home alone, I binge.

"I did not date much when I was younger, mainly because I was always the 'fat boy' in class. Frankly, I wouldn't know how to act with a woman, and I worry that if I was thin I might not be able to control my impulses. Maybe being overweight helps me control my emotions. Yes, I'd like to date someday, but even the thought makes me anxious. Dating would feel more out of control than eating! I'd rather avoid it. Eating is safer."

OUT OF CONTROL

All these people have something in common. They feel out of control when it comes to eating. Whether they binge or "graze" all day on food, hunger is not the issue. Eating is a result of an emotional emptiness or stress. Food compulsion is the accepted "addiction."

Food is everywhere, and eating is a national pastime. Food cannot be abstained from like other addictions. It has to be contended with on a daily basis. In other words, when food isn't in your body, it's in your face!

Food is used for celebration, special events, rewards and to numb and soothe emotional pain. People eat when they are happy, sad, angry, bored, restless, frustrated...well, you get the picture. Food and emotions are well-acquainted partners.

We socialize and relate to one another around food. "Let's get together for dinner."

"How about if we meet over coffee and bagels?" "Let's celebrate with a pizza party." "Can we have a spaghetti dinner fundraiser?" "I'm so upset. Pass the ice cream."

And the temptation to overindulge is all around us.

While temptation is all around, the perfect thin body is paraded and praised. On the one hand we are encouraged to overindulge, on the other, deny the temptation in order to look attractive. We're

Food compulsion is the accepted "addiction."

all a little nuts when it comes to weight and food!

Let's not forget that weight loss is big business in America. We'll do anything to shed those extra pounds—diet, take pills, rub on magical creams, drink disgusting shakes, endure liposuction or risk surgery. And yet, one in three, or 58 million, Americans ages twenty to seventy-four are overweight, and the numbers are increasing.[1] Childhood obesity is on the rise with 25 to 30 percent of children affected.[2]

So what can we do to break the cycle of bingeing and overeating? How can we stop the addiction we feel toward food? It's time to break the cycle of binge and compulsive overeating. In this book you will:

- Understand the dangers of compulsive overeating and binge eating

- Recognize the signs of compulsive and binge eating

- Decide if you have a problem

- Look at the causes of compulsive and binge eating

- Review biblical guidelines for healthy eating and self-control

- Practice break-free strategies that will help eliminate food compulsion

- Learn to live in freedom from the compulsion to overeat

Food does not have to rule your life. It's time to stop using food as a cure for emotional hunger and pain. Self-control is possible when the Holy Spirit lives within you. Freedom is not about testing your will power or finding a magical cure. It comes as you surrender your life to God, walk in

His ways and allow His Spirit to direct you. As the Spirit leads you, He will renew your mind, take control of your emotions and bring your will into obedience.

BREAKING FREE
PRAYER FOR YOU

Lord, I feel out of control when it comes to ever eating healthy. I confess I feel defeated by all my failures to lose weight when I've tried. I'm tired of even trying, but I want to break free from the food compulsion I feel. I need Your help.

CHAPTER 1

UNDERSTANDING COMPULSIVE AND BINGE EATING

The second day of a diet is always easier than the first. By the second day you're off it.
—JACKIE GLEASON

*H*ave you ever thought that your eating was impulsive and out of control? Do you dive into large quantities of food and not stop until you feel bloated or sick? Such is the case of a compulsive eater. Usually large amounts of high-calorie foods are consumed multiple times a day. The obvious result is weight gain. Thus compulsive overeaters are usually overweight or obese.

Perhaps you've tried skipping meals, fasting or dieting. But then the urge to eat overtakes you. You feel *addicted* to food, and the compulsion won't relent. The larger and more frustrated you become, the more you experience social withdrawal, depression, anxiety and panic attacks, work or school avoidance and loss of self-esteem.

Is Your Eating Compulsive?

If it seems your eating is compulsive, ask yourself these twenty-five questions:

1. Do I think about food often or even all the time?

2. Do I eat to relieve tension, stress, worry or upsets?

3. Do I eat when I'm bored?

4. Do I continue to eat after I feel full, sometimes to the point of feeling sick?

5. Does eating make me feel anxious?

6. Do I leave all my cares behind when I eat and try not to think about life's problems?

7. Do I cram in the food, feeling worried while I eat?

8. Do I have to clean my plate?

9. Do I eat in secret or hide food?

10. Do I eat quickly, shoving in the food?

11. Do I feel guilty after I eat?

12. Do I eat small portions in front of people, but go back for more food when people aren't around?

13. Do I binge (eat large amounts of food in a short period of time)?

14. Do I binge after I've tried to diet?

15. Can I eat one serving, or do I have to eat the entire amount (a bag of cookies, the half-gallon of ice cream)?

16. Do I feel out of control and impulsive?

17. Do I feel distressed over the way I eat?

18. Do I have impulse problems in other areas of my life (shopping, sex, gambling, alcohol or drugs)?

19. Do I eat often, even when I am not physically hungry?

20. Do people notice or tell me that I have an eating problem?

21. Do I lie to myself about how much I really eat?

22. Do I feel guilty and ashamed of my weight?

23. Do I have trouble tolerating negative feelings?

24. Have I been on numerous diets over the years?

25. Do I experience constant weight fluctuations?

If you answered *yes* to many of these questions, chances are you eat compulsively.

SIGNS OF COMPULSIVE EATING

Compulsive overeaters usually:

- Overeat due to emotional issues and stress, not because they are hungry

- Diet often because of guilt and weight gain

- Feel out of control when eating

- Feel disgusted with their bodies because they are overweight

- Binge eat or overeat throughout the day

BINGE EATING

Another type of compulsive eating is called *binge eating*. About 2 percent of the population binge eats.[1] Binge eating is similar to bulimia because it involves uncontrolled eating episodes (binges). The difference is compulsive binge eaters don't purge (get rid of the food by vomiting or taking laxatives). They eat until they are uncomfortably full. Most binge eaters are obese and struggle with weight fluctuations.

BREAKING F R E E

MENTAL HEALTH FACT

Do You Binge?

If you think you binge, look for these signs:[2]

- Do I have regular, recurrent binges?

- Do I feel out of control during a binge?

- Do I eat fast and feel uncomfortable?

- Do I eat large amounts of food when not physically hungry?

- Do I eat alone because I am embarrassed by how much I eat?

- Do I feel disgusted, guilty or depressed by the way I eat?

- Do I feel distressed by the above?

- Do I binge at least two days a week over a six-month period?

- Do I not engage in any kind of purging to get rid of the food?

The telltale sign of compulsive and binge eating is usually overweight or obesity. Both can lead to serious medical consequences. Overweight and obese people are often at higher risk for:

- Diabetes (Type II)
- Hypertension
- Dyslipidemia

- Stroke
- Cardiovascular disease
- Gallbladder disease
- Certain types of cancer
- Arthritis and gout
- Hernias, low back pain
- Gum disease
- Hypoxia
- Elevated cholesterol and triglyceride levels[3]

Psychologically, out-of-control eating can produce depression; anxiety; anger; fear; low self-esteem; hypersensitivity to criticism and approval; powerlessness; numbness; social preoccupation with food, weight and appearance; social withdrawal and isolation and secrecy from shame and guilt.

The social stigma associated with increased weight is incredible. Obese people are stereotyped and often viewed as ugly, lazy, unwanted, unhealthy, weak-willed or uncontrolled. If you are obese, you are less likely to marry and more likely to fall in social class. You are likely to be discriminated against concerning jobs, college entrance acceptance and to be stereotyped by your physician.[4] Basically you are stigmatized by an unsympathetic society; people are "allowed" to discriminate against you. Fat jokes abound.

WEIGHT GAIN

Most people classify obesity according to weight, even though there are numerous medical, psychological and behavioral variables involved. Obesity is referred to as a public health issue because of the associated medical complications leading to morbidity and mortality.

Obesity is *not* a psychological condition. It's a medical condition that has multiple causes, consequences and treatments. However, obesity can cause or be caused by emotional and social problems. And, as I've already stated, overweight and obesity are fallouts of compulsive overeating and bingeing.

Since a major concern associated with compulsive and binge eating is weight gain, let's understand more about it. Obviously, compulsive overeating without purging leads to weight gain. The goal is to eliminate the compulsion and learn to eat healthy. And you will probably need to lose weight. With years of failure behind you, don't give up. It is possible to get control and move into better health.

Since the extra weight is a health concern, let's first understand what constitutes overweight and obesity. Obesity is an excess of body fat. Little agreement exists on when body fat and weight become a health issue. In other words, what percentage of overweight puts you at risk? (Opinions range from 5 percent to 30 percent above ideal weight.) To make matters worse, a variety of tables are used to measure ideal weights.

Overweight and obesity are fallouts of compulsive overeating and bingeing.

Researchers use the Body Mass Index (BMI) as a measure of body fat and health risk. BMI is weight in kilograms per height in meters. The National Center for Health Statistics defines overweight as a BMI of 27.3 in women and 27.8 in men. This is approximately 20 percent to 40 percent above ideal weight on the 1983 Metropolitan Life tables.[5]

MEASURING OBESITY AND OVERWEIGHT

If I asked you to define obesity, most of you would give me a weight. In fact, each of us has a weight we try to avoid. But body fat is really more important than a number on the scale. Why? Because someone who is very muscular, with low body fat, would not be considered obese. But someone who is normal or underweight with an excess of body fat would be considered overweight.

Because so much of the population is overweight or obese, federal guidelines have been developed to assist physicians. These federal clinical practice guidelines help determine obesity. The experts have agreed on three measurements.[6]

Body Mass Index

The first measurement is the BMI (Body Mass Index) mentioned above. It's a bit complicated, but here is how you determine it. Multiply your weight in pounds by 703, and then divide it twice by your height in inches. For example, if you weight 135 pounds and are 5 feet 6 inches tall, multiply 135 x 703=94905, then divide 94905 by 66 inches=1437.95 and divide 1437.95 by 66 inches again to equal 21.78. Your BMI is 21.78. Overweight is defined by a BMI of 25 to 29.9, and obesity as a BMI of 30 or higher. These ranges are also in accord with the Dietary Guidelines for Americans established in 1995.

Waist circumference

The second measure is waist circumference. Why the waist? Because abdominal fat is usually a risk factor for disease. The way you figure the distribution of body fat around the waist is to take your waist measurement in inches and divide it by your hip size in inches. This gives you a ratio that needs to be below 0.8 for women and 1.0 for men. Higher ratios are associated with heart disease risk.[7] Here's an example: A woman with a 35-inch waist and 42-inch hips would have a ratio of 0.83 and be at risk.

Anthropometry

The third measure is called *anthropometry*, a skin-fold thickness taken from different points on the body—usually the triceps, shoulder blades and hips. Skin-fold thickness can help you know if weight is due to muscle or fat.

In addition to these measurements, physicians also evaluate you for other risk factors such as high cholesterol and blood pressure. So don't just look at the number on that dreaded scale. Based on these guidelines, there is much more to consider to determine your level of risk for health problems.

Now you may be thinking, *This is more information than I care to know*, but it is important to understand that weight concerns are about more than just pounds on the scale. Excess weight has physical, emotional, relational and spiritual consequences. We don't want to get so focused on weight gain that we ignore the real problem—the reasons for the compulsion and bingeing.

GET A PHYSICAL EXAMINATION

Your first step to break free from compulsive overeating requires a step of courage. Schedule a complete physical examination. I know you hate the idea and don't want to face the scale and the doctor's reaction to your weight. But it is important to make sure you don't have a metabolic disturbance such as diabetes or thyroid disease that may be contributing to your weight problem. Find a physician who has compassion for eating disorders and won't ridicule you or hand you a twelve-hundred-calorie diet and expect will power to be the solution.

Your first step to break free from compulsive overeating requires a step of courage. Schedule a complete physical examination.

Meet with a physician who will monitor your physical health and encourage you to deal with the underlying emotional issues related to compulsive eating. If your doctor tells you that it is unsafe to maintain your present weight, listen to this advice.

Then begin to address what causes the

eating disorder. Once you address the reasons for the compulsive behavior, you can deal with your excess weight. Trying to lose weight before you deal with the compulsion is a setup for failure. Once you gain control over the compulsion, you will stop gaining weight. In the meantime, make sure someone monitors your medical condition.

The Causes for Compulsive and Binge Eating

If engaging in compulsive and binge eating leads to negative consequences like weight gain and increased health risks, why do we do them? Well, that's the big question, isn't it?

The reasons for compulsive eating are numerous and vary from person to person. There is no one cause, but there is a common thread—food fills an emotional emptiness and is used to soothe, numb and escape emotional feelings. You may be someone who had childhood hurts and rejections, and thus food is your friend. Or perhaps you had a loving family but experienced trauma, and food was used to comfort and calm you.

People overeat for all kinds of reasons. A small percentage of people have medical problems that relate to overeating and obesity. Most people, however, overeat out of emotional distress. You may eat when you are bored, stressed, sad, depressed, anxious, angry, hurt, happy or for any other emotional reason. Food can be a way to celebrate or soothe and numb you from a bad experience.

BREAKING F R E E

MENTAL HEALTH FACT

Why Do You Eat?

If you are a compulsive or binge eater, you may eat for these reasons. Check this list and see if any of these apply to you.

You...

- Have difficulty identifying hunger, emotions and other bodily states

- Have difficulty regulating feelings, and food is used to calm or numb those feelings

- Use food to soothe relationship rejections

- Use food as a source of peace and calm, a self-medication against pain

- Use food as a substitute for emotional emptiness and gratification

- Use food as a substitute for love and affection

- Eat to punish yourself for past mistakes

- Keep people at a distance by overeating, especially when it comes to dealing with issues of sexuality

- Have a history of repeated losses

- Use food as a way of rebellion to other tightly controlled areas of your life

- Eat for immediate gratification

- Have significant fears of abandonment

- Eat to avoid intimacy

- Worry that if you lose weight, you may not be able to control other impulses like sexual feelings

- Use food for relaxation

- Use food to swallow angry feelings

- Use food to hide a fear of failure ("If I were thin, I would...")

Food can be chosen as a comforting or numbing agent for relationship pain. You may be hurt by a divorce, a cruel father, a betraying friend, a mean-spirited boss or any number of other people. Instead of drinking, getting high, shopping or gambling, you escape through food—the one sanctioned *addiction*. Or you may overeat and have other addiction problems.

The bottom line is that food is not used as nourishment and sustenance but to fill some emotional emptiness or calm anxiety. According to the members of my compulsive overeating groups, "Food is always available, never talks back to me, tastes good and gives immediate pleasure. Food is my friend; it comforts and soothes me when no one else will. That's why it's hard to give up."

BREAKING 🕊 FREE

PRAYER FOR YOU

Lord, I admit food has been my friend. I use it to feel better for the moment, but then in the long run I hate how I feel; nothing really changes except I've gotten fatter. I need to change this and get control.

CHAPTER 2

DIETS AND WEIGHT-LOSS METHODS

The biggest seller is cookbooks and the second is diet books— how not to eat what you've just learned how to cook.

—ANDY ROONEY

*D*ieting is one of the most common ways eating problems develop. You overeat, gain weight, feel guilty, diet, lose a few pounds, then lose control over eating and gain even more weight! The cycle seems never ending and is very discouraging. Dieting only deals with symptoms (weight gain). It doesn't address the problem. And if you are a compulsive overeater, you've tried every diet known to man with no lasting result.

Compulsive overeating is a habit that must be broken. To begin, forget your dieting history. The solution isn't a diet, especially all the fad ones you've tried. It's learning to manage your emotions in a healthy way and not using food to fill emotional emptiness. Stop saying you can't get control. You can. It just takes making changes and allowing the Holy Spirit to empower you.

Let's face it. Food is soothing and tastes good. As I mentioned before, compulsive overeaters feel there is nothing better than food! It is always available, not illegal, can't talk back, provides immediate gratification, gives pleasure, smells good, tastes good and is enjoyable. But you have to be willing to give it up and learn new ways to cope. You can do it! But I won't lie and tell you it's easy.

Deal with both the excess weight gain and the compulsion.

Don't make the mistake of focusing only on weight gain and ignoring the emotional reasons behind the gain. Deal with both the excess weight gain and the compulsion.

Let's begin with the compulsion. A compulsive-eating problem is not exactly the same as a drug or alcohol problem. You can't abstain from food, and you aren't physiologically addicted when you eat. Overeating doesn't involve chemically altering substances that result in tolerance and withdrawal symptoms. Some would argue that food chemically alters the brain and affects mood. While it is true that nutrition impacts the brain and mood, it doesn't alter your state of consciousness like other substances. But food can become a psychological addiction. It can be a learned response to emotional stress and negative life experiences. The good news is that if it is learned, it can be unlearned.

Break-free strategies will include learning other coping skills, substituting new behaviors for overeating and identifying the triggers to overeating. In addition, you will have to develop good eating habits, along with good nutrition and exercise. Sorry, there are no shortcuts.

Biology Matters

Biology influences our size and weight.

21

There is a relationship between the weight of biological parents and the weight of their children. If you have obese parents, you have a greater chance of being overweight. Remember, though, that eating habits are learned in families as well. So if your parents are compulsive overeaters, you may have learned compulsive habits as well.

Metabolism and growth patterns also influence weight and are genetically influenced. Fat cells multiply at three important times in our development—before birth and during infancy and adolescence. These three periods of development can be times when fat cells are also added because of overeating.

What's important about this brief note on biology is that your weight is influenced by genetic factors. This doesn't mean you are doomed to be overweight because of it, but genetics do play a role in metabolism, body composition and more.

Your weight history is important to consider. If you've been overweight all your life, currently weighing 280 pounds, for example, and you want to weigh 120 pounds, you may be setting yourself up for failure. If your lowest adult weight was 180 pounds, a more realistic goal may be 200 pounds. When unrealistic expectations aren't met, it's a setup for overeating again. You feel failed. The food is used to soothe those feelings of failure.

Weight-Loss Questions to Ask Yourself

Here are some important questions to ask in terms of deciding how difficult weight loss will be:

1. *Have you been overweight since childhood?* If so, it may be harder for you to lose weight than someone whose weight gain began in adulthood. You have more years of habit to undo.

2. *Are other people in your family overweight?* If they are, you could have inherited a biological predisposition to weight gain. On the

other hand, you may have a family of compulsive overeaters who have learned how to use food for comfort. Either way, it will require effort to make changes.

3. *Do you have any underlying disease state like hypothyroidism or Cushing's syndrome that is the cause of weight gain?* Check with your doctor and have that physical examination I mentioned.

4. *How overweight are you?* The more you have to lose, the more discouraging it can be to stay with your plan and new habits. Support is needed.

5. *Are you realistic about how much weight you have to lose and how long it may take to do it safely?* Begin by setting the weight loss goal at 10 percent of your current body weight. Consider weight loss of one to two pounds a week as successful.

6. *Do you binge, deny how much you eat or tend to make excuses for overeating?* If you do any of the above, don't start a weight-loss program until you can be

honest about your behavior. Otherwise, you'll fail, and you don't need that.

7. *Do you have people who will support your efforts?* Social support is critical when you make changes in eating habits. Spouses and family members can sabotage your efforts.

8. *Are you willing to make lifelong changes and give up dieting?* Weight loss isn't a time-limited deal. You are committing to change the way you think, feel and behave.

9. *If you never dropped a pound, would you still be a worthwhile person?* If your feelings of worth are tied to your weight, you are not healed. Jesus loves you unconditionally. He esteems you regardless of your weight. Get a revelation of His love for you.

10. *Do you want to change?* Are you ready to give up these destructive habits? Change doesn't come quickly, but if you are committed to the goal of getting control over the eating, you

will be successful. You will need patience and the ability to recognize the small but important changes you make.[1]

WEIGHT-LOSS METHODS

By now I hope you understand that gaining control over the compulsive eating is your first goal. More help to accomplish this goal is found in chapter five. Second, you must learn to eat healthy. Since so many people struggling with weight issues wonder about the plethora of weight-loss methods, let's take a look at these. I am not making recommendations. I just want you to be aware of the basic pros and cons of going these routes. These strategies should be discussed with a physician and dietitian.

Pills and medications

We are a pill-popping society. When we feel bad, we take something to feel better. Americans are in love with drug solutions to anything. Pill popping is easy, convenient and doesn't make us deal with the complicated issues of life. Temporary relief is the goal.

This pill-popping mentality is all around us. On the one hand we tell our children and teens not to take illegal drugs or misuse medications. On the other hand, we model the opposite by popping a pill for every ache and pain. Nowhere is the quick-fix mentality more evident than when you look at weight-loss products. The number of products on the market claiming to make you lose weight is staggering. I am amazed at what people will swallow to reach the thin ideal of American beauty. Billions of dollars are wasted on elusive promises to melt away pounds. We covet the magic pill, and we'll try anything in an effort to find it.

At present there is no magic pill. We are still searching for a better understanding of the molecular biology of obesity. If we truly understood the causes of obesity, we could do more than treat the symptoms. But until that happens, pharmacological solutions for obesity remain hopeful but not yet proven.

Science continues to bring us new treatments, but we need proof of their effectiveness. Remember the fenfluramine hydrochloride and dexfenfluramine hydrochloride fiasco. Wyeth-Ayerst Laboratories in Philadelphia, Pennsylvania, the American distributor of fenfluramine and dexfenfluramine, voluntarily withdrew these medications from the market in September 1997 at the request of the Food and Drug Administration.

Then there was phen-fen (phentermine and fenfluramine). Obese patients were flocking to physicians for phen-fen prescriptions. People were desperate to find the right combination of drugs to make those pounds drop. At the height of the phen-fen popularity, I was working with an internist who studied the research of Michael Weintraub and colleagues at the University of Rochester in New York. The results indicated these medications were less than exciting in the long run. Then national concern about possible serious side effects related to valvular heart disease surfaced. People who jumped on the phen-fen bandwagon were left wondering what damage, if any, they may have done to their physical bodies. And, over time, many patients gained back most of their weight loss.

Since that time, newer agents have been approved, including sibutramine and orlistat. Again, time and research will tell if long-term results can be maintained without significant risks. The question continues to be, What amount of sustained weight loss is considered successful and worth the risks? Is a 5 percent reduction in weight worth the long-term effects of continued drug use?

After the 1994 discovery of the ob gene and its protein product leptin, the search goes on. The hope is that pharmacology will eventually cure obesity. Even as I write this book, an exciting new hormone discovery has been made that may boost weight loss. A hormone that is naturally produced in the intestines (called PYY-36) has been shown to reduce food intake in rats.[2]

The wish of many is that a magic pill will be discovered and our obesity problems solved. In the meantime, keep doing the sensible things we know to do: Eat healthy, exercise and change your lifestyle. It may be awhile.

Very low-calorie diets

The popularity of very low-calorie diets (VLCDs) was enormous in the 1980s. Remember Oprah strutting her thin and trim body on TV? If you've tuned in recently, you won't see the Oprah of the VLCD era. You'll see an attractive woman who struggles with her weight just like the rest of us. So what are we to think of these VLCDs as a weight-loss option for the significantly obese person?

Keep doing the sensible things we know to do: Eat healthy, exercise and change your lifestyle.

VLCDs were defined in 1979 by a scientific panel as fewer than eight hundred kilocalories daily. A revision of that definition includes ten kilocalories per kilogram of ideal body weight. The revision takes into account energy requirements related to body size.[3]

The modern versions of VLCDs are considered generally safe if used under a physician's care. There are no increased mortality rates associated with their use. These diets are recommended for people who are at least 30 percent overweight and who undergo a thorough medical examination. Contraindications for use are recent myocardial infarction; a cardiac condition disorder; a history of cerebrovascular, renal or hepatic disease; cancer; Type I diabetes; pregnancy; bulimia nervosa; significant depression; acute psychiatric illness and substance abuse disorders (excluding cigarette smoking).[4] But always check with your physician when even considering something like VLCDs.

The attractions to VLCDs include rapid weight loss and the simplicity of eating. With liquid diets, there are no choices—food is avoided. The downside is that these diets are a temporary solution to weight loss. They don't teach one how to modify lifestyle despite the frequent use of a behavioral psychologist who instructs patients to modify eating habits and exercise. Many patients go off the VLCDs and eat as they did prior to the diet. Of course, weight comes back. And when you reintroduce food back into your diet, the compulsion is often still there and not treated.

In the short term, patients on VLCDs lose weight. Any weight-loss effort, though, must take into account weight-loss maintenance. According to data compiled by obesity researcher Tom Wadden, patients on VLCDs regain 35 percent to 50 percent of their lost weight in the year following treatment. Only 10 percent to 20 percent maintain their weight losses that first year, and an equal number regain it all. Over time, patients gain increasing amounts of weight.[5]

Considering the time (medical monitoring and groups) and expense of VLCDs ($2,500 and up for a twenty-six-week program), the benefits are questionable. The use of VLCDs needs to be reevaluated. If the long-term results are no better than traditional reducing diets, what's the point? In fact, the sense of failure many patients feel after losing a chunk of weight only to regain it is demoralizing. Too much time, effort and money were spent on something that didn't demonstrate long-time staying power. You have to decide if it's worth it.

Surgery

Surgical treatment for obesity may be recommended for people whose obesity is refractory or who have obesity-related conditions that pose serious health consequences. Surgical intervention is usually reserved for those with a BMI (body mass index) of 40 or greater, or a BMI of at least 35 with obesity-related health conditions.

Surgery can achieve maintainable losses of 40 percent to 60 percent of pre-surgery weight.[6] But weight loss is a complicated psychological as well as physical feat. Unfortunately, the psychological state of a patient is not always considered when recommending this option. Increasingly, more surgeons are interested in psychological screenings for medically qualified patients. Unfortunately, far too many surgeries are still performed without taking this necessary step.

Positive personality changes can accompany weight loss.[7] Patients often report feeling less helpless, more stable, have improved mood and so on. Other patients experience negative psychological postoperative changes.[8]

I've had patients who experienced a rise in anxiety because of trauma histories. When pounds are dropped, they feel vulnerable and scared. If fear and anxiety were channeled through food, and food is no longer available as a coping mechanism, problems can arise.

Others have spent years fighting social discrimination, attacks on self-esteem and rejection and view surgery as a way to gain an acceptable body. When the physical body conforms to social expectation, the attention can be overwhelming and difficult to handle.

Furthermore, many obese patients do not know how to determine their internal emotional states. They often see all needs as hunger needs. Emotional-based eating does not go away with surgical weight loss.

The key, then, is to be screened for psychological issues *prior* to surgery and address any potential negative outcomes. It appears that those who do best with weight reduction via surgical treatment are those who are

Emotional-based eating does not go away with surgical weight loss.

psychologically healthy and make this decision with the recommendation of their physician for medical reasons.

New developments continue to be reported in the field of obesity and weight loss. This is exciting, but the psychological issues have to be treated no matter how weight loss is achieved. Controlling the compulsive behavior is key. Emotionally, we have to learn not to use food as our nurturer. Spiritually, we must be filled with the power of the Holy Spirit.

PRAYER FOR YOU

Lord, I look at all these options and feel overwhelmed. Am I hoping there will be some magical way to make the weight disappear and get my eating under control? If I am, help me see the core issues involved—that freedom is more than just a weight-loss method and that I need to address the emotional reasons for overeating as well.

CHAPTER 3

BIBLICAL HELP AND GUIDELINES

Don't gobble your food, don't talk with your mouth full. And don't stuff yourself...

PROVERBS 23:2-3,
THE MESSAGE

*E*ating and drinking are often referenced in biblical life. People gathered together to celebrate and fellowship around food. For example, Jesus ate with His disciples, shared a meal with Lazarus, and Martha cooked Him a meal. There are numerous accounts of people sharing meals and dining together. The same is still true today. It is not a sin to enjoy a good meal. But there is a difference between enjoyment and eating compulsively.

Gluttony As Rebellion

According to Webster's dictionary, a *glutton* is someone who eats excessively or greatly desires something. In the Bible, gluttony is referenced with rebellion, drunkenness and stubbornness. "And they

When you don't exercise restraint over indulgences, the consequences are negative.

shall say to the elders of his city, 'This son of ours is stubborn and rebellious; he will not obey our voice; he is a glutton and a drunkard'" (Deut. 21:20, NKJV). This scripture is talking about rebellion. Have you ever thought of overeating as rebellious? Search your heart and ask, "Do I eat when I'm angry or when I feel rebellious?"

Perhaps you are compliant on the outside, always doing what you are told or going with the flow, but secretly harbor feelings of anger and resentment that get swallowed with food. Compulsive overeating can be an indirect way to rebel. Here's an example. You worked very hard to complete a project at work. The project required a great deal of time and effort, but the end result was excellent. Your boss took a look at it, tossed it aside and told you to rework it. All you felt was anger, but you didn't express it directly. Instead, you left work at 5:00 P.M. and binged on the way home. You swallowed the anger, never confronted your boss and continued to feel out of control. That "out-of-control" feeling found expression in compulsive overeating, an out-of-control behavior.

GLUTTONY AND POVERTY

Proverbs 23 is a chapter about exercising restraint. In Proverbs 23:21, the outcome of gluttony is poverty: "For drunkards and gluttons become poor, and drowsiness clothes them in rags." *The Message* says, "Drunks and gluttons will end up on skid row, in a stupor and dressed in rags." In other words, when you don't exercise restraint over indulgences, the consequences are negative.

Gluttony As a Negative
Behavioral Trait

In Matthew 11:19, Jesus mentioned that people tried to discredit Him as the Messiah by making reference to Him as a glutton. Gluttony is a negative behavioral trait associated with someone who won't exercise restraint. Not only was Jesus misunderstood by the religious leaders of His day, but they accused Him of being a lush because of His "feasting." "The Son of Man came eating and drinking, and they say, 'Here is a glutton and a drunkard, a friend of tax collectors and "sinners."' But wisdom is proved right by her actions" (Matt. 11:19).

Desire for food can be greater than our desire for the things of God. When this happens, food becomes an idol. And when constant thoughts about food affect our functioning and relationships, it becomes a source of worry and anxiety.

Matthew 6:25 specifically tells us not to worry about what we eat or drink or about our bodies. Why? Because eating is a need that God will supply—He made provision in the Garden, gave instructions for the food supply in the ark, rained down food from heaven in the wilderness and fed the very hungry five thousand with loaves and fishes. Throughout the Bible, God supplied food to sustain and nourish His own. And His promises are the same yesterday, today and forever.

In addition to meeting our physical needs, God wants to satisfy our spiritual appetite as well. In John 6:35 He calls Himself the "bread of life." Whoever comes to Him will never be thirsty or hungry again. What a promise! He will fulfill *all* our longings and hunger.

Nothing will satisfy that empty place but an intimate relationship with Jesus Christ. No matter how you try to fill the void—with food, drink, drugs, gambling, shopping, glamour or other things—only God will satisfy in the long term. Other things provide instant gratification, but the desire for more won't be satiated.

Let God Fill the Void

How do you overcome the craving for

food? Stop looking to anyone or anything else to affirm who you are or to give you approval. Develop an intimate relationship with God. He already loves you, but He desires to really know you. Allow God to communicate with you, to lead and direct you, and to use your gifts. If you search for satisfaction elsewhere, you'll come up empty. It's time to get personal. Don't just learn about God—experience Him. You need the power of the Holy Spirit to help you overcome the temptation to overeat.

Food is not the solution for the emptiness you feel. The enemy lies to you. He tells you to fill that void with anything but God because he knows that when God takes control of your life, he's lost control over you. He wants you struggling, captive and trying to free yourself in your own power.

Admit that you've lost control. Ask God to take over and empower you. Then cooperate with the process by exercising spiritual discipline. Daily fill yourself full of the Word of God. Spend time in prayer and regular communication with God.

Allow the Holy Spirit to move through you by removing roadblocks to intimacy such as unconfessed sin and unhealthy guilt and shame. Resolve issues from your past, and heal old wounds that have kept you captive.

Face the hurt and pain of your life. Don't avoid it, eat it away or try to numb it. God will give you the grace to move

Food is not the solution for the emptiness you feel.

through the pain. Then He can fill your emptiness with His joy and love.

DEVELOP SELF-CONTROL

God wants balance in your life. This requires moderation in a number of areas; one of them is eating. However, our culture promotes the opposite. We are encouraged to self-indulge and engage in anything that brings us pleasure. Immediate gratification is the postmodern mantra. "Buy that expensive car you can't afford. It will make you feel important." "Treat yourself to a night out. After all, you deserve it." "Have sex when the moment feels right because the opportunity may be lost forever." "Overindulge!" Food is no exception.

With the culture screaming, "Indulge, satisfy, gratify," how do you exercise self-control? It's extremely difficult even without an eating problem. But your hope is in God. He promised you can have it.

Galatians 5:22–23 says, "But the fruit of the Spirit is love, joy, peace, patience, kindness, goodness, faithfulness, gentleness and self-control." According to this passage, fruit is produced in the life of a Christian. The seed is the Word of God. You plant the seed (the Word) in your heart first. The result of knowing and believing God's Word is self-control or, said another way, the result of planting the seed is fruit (self-control).

Because we love God, we want to please Him and keep His commands. As we become obedient to His plan, His way of living and His will, these things produce self-discipline. Self-discipline entails practicing self-control in all areas of our lives.

This may mean changing your behavior

and addressing areas you previously denied or numbed out with food. As you practice self-control and please God with your lifestyle, He gives supernatural control. Then it is possible to be self-disciplined with food. Remember when we are weak, He makes us strong. Our strength doesn't come from will power but from the Spirit working in us.

In the natural it is hard to exercise self-control. We try, but often fail. Then, we get discouraged, and the enemy comes in and tells us to give up. His voice says, "Forget it. It's too hard. You can't do it. Just give in." Remember, he tried this with Jesus.

When Jesus was led into the wilderness by the Spirit, He fasted. As a result, He was hungry and tired when the devil approached and tempted Him. Interestingly, one of Jesus' temptations involved food. (So did the original temptation.)

Satan's strategy—tempt Jesus to change the rules and reach His goals through a shortcut. Turn the stone into bread, and Satan would give Him the kingdoms of this world. Since Satan has dominion over the world, he had bargaining power. If Jesus gave in to the temptation, Satan would rule over Him. Thankfully, Jesus didn't opt for a shortcut, but fulfilled His mission as our blood sacrifice for the atonement of sin. Because He was obedient unto death, we can be saved and have the power to overcome temptation.

Compulsive eating is giving in to the shortcut. The craving is satisfied in the short term, but the cost is high in the long term. As you give in to momentary pleasure or the numbing ability of food, you suffer the guilt of unrestrained eating; you momentarily avoid emotional pain but are left with accompanying weight gain.

Trust God to help you resolve interpersonal problems, negative feelings about your body and esteem.

As you identify the specific issues involved in overeating, you can understand why self-control is so difficult. You have to face those issues, not deny them with food compulsion. This can create anxiety. It's easier to overeat than feel emotional pain.

So work out all your issues associated with overeating while filling up with God's Word. It produces fruit, specifically self-control. Determine to face the pain of your past or present situations. Jesus wants to heal you. Trust God to help you resolve interpersonal problems, negative feelings about your body and esteem. Tackle the root causes noted in chapter one. Trust God to give you the courage to face those parts of you that need changing.

BREAKING FREE

PRAYER FOR YOU

Lord, I realize I am powerless without You empowering me to overcome. I desperately need Your help. I will commit to spiritual discipline—read my Bible, pray regularly and praise and worship You. You promise to give me self-control as I walk in obedience to You. I pray now that You will give me what I need to have victory over this compulsion.

CHAPTER 4

WHERE TO BEGIN

Chains of habit are too light to be felt until they are too heavy to be broken.

—WARREN BUFFET

*T*he first step is to break the compulsive eating and/or binge behavior. Later you can focus on losing weight. Begin by asking yourself this question, "Do I know the difference between physical hunger and emotional hunger?"

When you haven't eaten for a period of time, you experience hunger pains. The stomach contracts, and the brain signals you to eat. Compulsive or binge eating isn't a reaction to physiological hunger. Instead, it's a learned response to emotions and stress. Food is used to relieve or numb out emotional pain. Over time you've developed the habit of using food to calm down, celebrate, deal with anger and so on. When depression and stress hits, bingeing or compulsive eating goes into autopilot. In other words, the learned response kicks in.

Whenever you feel like overeating or bingeing, decide, "Will I give in to this learned behavior, or will I try to deal with my emotions some other way?" In order to make this decision, think about when you last ate and how much you ate. True hunger usually doesn't set in for a number of hours. Most Americans have no idea what hunger really feels like. In most cases, physical hunger isn't motivating you to eat. You are probably feeling emotionally empty or upset. Choose not to respond to those feelings with food. Instead, substitute another behavior. (See chapter five.)

IDENTIFY OVEREATING TRIGGERS

If you know you aren't physically hungry, then try to determine what emotion or stress event is tempting you to overeat. Stress and upsets are called *emotional triggers*. A trigger is a cue that *precedes* the binge or compulsive eating. Try to identify the trigger. What happened right before you overate? Was it an argument with your spouse, anger, a commercial about food or the smell of a cake baking in the oven? Something cued your desire to overeat. These cues or triggers can be situations or emotions. Many times we are unaware of them. We don't think about what happened before we overate.

Emotional Food Triggers

The cycle usually goes like this:

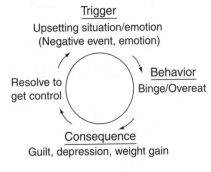

Trigger
Upsetting situation/emotion
(Negative event, emotion)

Behavior
Binge/Overeat

Resolve to
get control

Consequence
Guilt, depression, weight gain

You can interrupt this cycle of bingeing and overeating by changing the triggers (situations, emotions), the behavior (binge, overeat) or both. When possible, change the situation. If, for example, you binge every time you go to an all-you-can-eat buffet, stop going. Go to a restaurant with a sit-down menu. You won't eat as much if you have to pay for every item. Choose restaurants with healthy food selections instead of high-fat, high-cholesterol meals.

Or instead of changing the situation, you can change your reaction to a situation or emotion. If you overeat every time you feel angry, you can work on a new response to angry feelings. Anger isn't something you can avoid feeling for the rest of your life. The better idea is to find a way to feel angry and not overeat.

The chart on page 53 will help you to chart these triggers so you can become aware of them.

When you keep track of overeating triggers (situation and emotions), you begin to see a pattern over time. For example, you might notice that every time you have a disagreement with your mother-in-law, you binge. This information is helpful in making changes. You can either stop having disagreements with your mother-in-law (not a likely solution) or find a new way to behave when this happens (a better plan). Chapter five will provide you with suggestions for new ways to respond.

Keep a Food Journal

Next, keep a food journal. In my experience treating compulsive overeating, most people grossly underestimate the amount of calories eaten in any given day. They didn't remember tasting five spoonfuls of chili while cooking it, or they forgot about the candy bar they grabbed while paying for gas. Impulsive eating is so automatic that it happens without thought. Writing down every food item that goes in your mouth for a two-week period can be an eye opener. I suggest you try it.

A food journal also helps you take a look at eating habits you've developed. Do you hit the fast-food joints regularly during the week? Eat in the car? Do you skip

	TRACKING YOUR EMOTIONAL TRIGGERS		
Situation	Emotion	Behavior	Rating (1–10)
What was happening before I overate?	What emotion did I feel?	What did I do? (binge or overeat)	How strongly did I feel it?

breakfast, barely eat lunch and then binge from dinner on through the night? If so, changes need to be made in your eating habits. Don't skip breakfast, or any meal times for that matter. Adding two snacks a day between meals is also a good idea. Regular scheduled eating helps prevent bingeing.

A food journal helps you take a look at eating habits you've developed.

You may need to work with a registered dietitian on meal planning and food choices. The idea is to develop good eating habits for life and to give up dieting. Healthy eating is a lifestyle, not something you do until you lose X number of pounds. There are no "bad" foods, but there certainly are good and bad choices in terms of portions and nutrition.

Some people have to learn portion control. My favorite dietitian uses food models to teach this. Her patients are usually shocked when they see how small a standard "portion" is for a meat or other food item. It'll make you think about what is served in many restaurants. You may have to cut down on portion size, not cut out certain foods.

Another area to examine is your nutrition. Americans tend to eat high-fat, high-sugar, processed foods without much nutritional value. We've given in to fast food, eating on the run and grabbing whatever is convenient because of our lifestyles. The result is that we eat a lot of empty calories, which don't sustain good health and energy levels. And because of these bad habits, our children aren't getting the nutrients they need for proper growth and development.

Write down when, where, how much and what you ate. Again, you'll begin to see patterns that need change. You'll find, over time, that you can eat well and be satisfied. And you'll learn to eat at the appropriate times and places instead of eating compulsively and impulsively.

The purpose of journaling isn't to make you feel bad or guilty, but to help you realistically see what you've eaten over a period of time. It's harder to deny overeating when you've recorded every bite. In so many cases, people skip meals, eat in front of the television set, grab fast food and set themselves up for bingeing. A dietitian can help you establish regular eating times, healthy meal portions and eating habits.

The constant cycle of dieting, failing and then compulsively eating gets replayed and needs to be interrupted. There is no easy way around learning good eating habits. You have to practice until new habits are developed. The key is not to give in to discouragement. Stay firm in your resolve to change unhealthy patterns, but don't expect it to happen overnight. Change takes time.

SET REALISTIC SHORT-TERM GOALS

One of the fastest ways to become discouraged is to expect change quickly. So many of my clients begin the hard work I'm describing and give up the first time they mess up. Failure is so familiar. It's like an old friend that won't go away. Don't give up. Change usually comes in increments.

Unrealistic goals are a setup for failure.

Food Journal

Where I Ate	Time of Day	Portion Size	Food Eaten
Ex: In the car	11:00 A.M.	Oversized French Fries (binge or overeat)	French Fries and Coke snack
Ex: Buffet	6:00 P.M.	All you can eat, 3 helpings of each food	Mashed potatoes, gravy, roast beef, beans in sauce, rolls, pie and ice cream, Coke, salad with 4 tablespoons of salad dressing

57

If, for example, your compulsive overeating has led to a one-hundred-pound weight gain, it's unrealistic to expect a one-hundred-pound weight loss in the next few months. A more realistic goal would be to aim for a 10 percent weight reduction over a reasonable period of time (six months to a year). Again, work with a dietitian to set realistic weight-loss goals. The weight doesn't come flying off for most people. And maintaining that weight loss is the important part. It requires a change in lifestyle.

Stay firm in your resolve to change unhealthy patterns, but don't expect it to happen overnight. Change takes time.

Make your goals reachable and short term. For example, instead of saying, "I won't binge for a week," say, "My goal is not to binge today." Each small success builds confidence. You should expect to fail every now and then. Most successes don't come in a straight line. You fall, get back up and keep moving forward.

EXERCISE

Most overweight people know they should exercise but don't want to do it. For one thing, exercise hurts when you are significantly overweight. And who wants to put on those exercise clothes and parade your body in front of a bunch of glamour exercise queens? But in a moment of resolve, you joined a health club and spent big money on a membership you couldn't afford and never use. Then, feeling failed and financially broke, you gave up on the whole idea of exercise.

Don't give up on exercise; just rethink it. Exercise is a *lifestyle*, not an activity you do to lose weight. You don't have to join a gym, spend a lot of money or commit to running the marathon! Just begin by walking short distances or making small changes like parking your car farther away from the mall door so you have to walk a longer distance. Take the stairs instead of the elevator. Lose the TV remote and change channels by getting up out of your chair. Make small changes that add up to big improvements over time.

Make your goals small and reachable in order to build on feelings of success. It's too easy to be defeated by lofty goals that seem impossible to reach. Think one step at a time, a day at a time. It took you months or years to develop bad habits; therefore, it will take you time to change them. Give yourself a break!

PREVENTION: A WORD TO PARENTS ABOUT CHILDHOOD OBESITY

Childhood obesity is increasing. About 25–30 percent of children in the United States are overweight according to physician Rebecca Moran.[1] Obesity not only creates psychological burdens but also medical dangers such as diabetes, gallbladder disease, sleep apnea and a worsening of asthma.

No parent wants his or her child to suffer the cruel teasing that often comes from being overweight. And certainly no one wishes for her child to develop the destructive path of an eating disorder. However, emotional damage is often inflicted on overweight children. The pain involves self-hatred that can lead to depression and anxiety, social isolation and alienation.

So what can you do to help an overweight child deal with her feelings of self-hate and the reactions of people around her? Early intervention of a problem saves a lot of heartache.

Once you recognize the signs of an eating problem, do something. Don't minimize the problem or hope it will magically disappear. The eating behavior is usually a sign that

The major reasons for childhood obesity are overeating, inadequate exercise and eating disorders.

something in your child's or teen's life is problematic and needs attention.

The major reasons for childhood obesity are overeating, inadequate exercise and eating disorders. Hormonal and genetic causes do exist, but they are the rare exceptions. Even though most cases of overweight are not medically based, it's a good idea to see your doctor for a complete physical examination to rule out a metabolic disturbance such as diabetes or thyroid disorder.

Next, deal with whatever relationship and emotional issues are upsetting your child. For example, is your child going through a difficult time due to divorce? Are expectations realistic? Are you critical of your child's appearance, making verbal digs at weight and eating? Do you single her out in front of others? Are you constantly talking about *diet*? Has there been abuse or trauma such as date rape?

Then think about four main areas of your child's life that could be connected with food:

- How does she fit in *socially*? Is she anxious, uncomfortable and avoiding others? Does she eat because of this anxiety?

- Are there *opportunities* to overeat? Are meal times unscheduled with family members going and coming? Is the house filled with high-fat, empty-calorie snacks? Is snacking an all-day thing? Do parents overeat and model poor nutrition in food choices?

- Does your child or teen *think negative thoughts* about herself? Does she verbalize regular put-downs? Is she talking a lot about her imperfect body?

- Is she reacting to *physical discomfort* by eating? Is she eating to relieve headaches or to cope with feeling tired? Has she had a chronic illness and is now using food to comfort?

Don't assume your child is doing well because her grades are good or she smiles and tells you everything is fine. Talk about what it is like to be overweight in terms of friends and school. Offer to help learn healthy eating guidelines and develop a more active lifestyle.

Of course, the best advice I can give is to *prevent* childhood obesity. Beginning in infancy, parents need to accurately read their babies' hunger cues.

As a child grows, help her eat well. Don't skip meals. Have regular snack times. This prevents the urge to binge.

As the teen years approach, guide your child with healthy food choices. It's OK to eat a fast-food double cheeseburger, but a steady diet of them is not a good idea. Discourage dieting. It's one of the most common entrées into an eating disorder.

The emotional and spiritual life of any child is key. Know your child. Stop your busy schedule and pay attention to what she feels and thinks. It's your job to impart the Word of God and to help her find her true identity in Christ. Begin early.

Finally, check your own attitudes about body image and weight. Do you obsess over your imperfections or define yourself by appearance? Do you

It's your job to impart the Word of God and to help her find her true identity in Christ.

have a strong sense of self based on God's Word and calling in your life? Are you a healthy role model when it comes to handling difficult emotions and relationships? Does your child see the Word of God applied daily in your life? If you can't answer *yes* to most of these questions, then start making changes now.

BREAKING FREE

PRAYER FOR YOU

Lord, I want to be honest about what goes in my mouth and how much I eat. I also want to become aware of what triggers overeating and make changes. Show me these things so I can honestly face what needs to change. With Your help, I can make necessary changes.

BREAK-FREE STRATEGIES

> *Dieting: A system of starving yourself to death so you can live a little longer.*
>
> —JAN MURRAY

IDENTIFY FEELINGS

Compulsive overeating and bingeing have everything to do with feelings. First, identify the emotion you feel when you have the urge to overeat. Do you feel tired, bored, angry, frustrated, rejected, hurt, happy, depressed or anxious? Feelings or emotions cue overeating or bingeing. Therefore, we must learn to identify those feelings and then manage them apart from food. Easier said then done!

Once you've identified your feelings, the next step is to express them directly rather than medicating them with food. Here are a few ideas that might help.

1. *Talk out your feelings with someone*—a friend, a counselor, spouse or trusted adult. Find someone you trust who will listen to you. Women in particular feel better when they can talk out a problem.

2. *Write down your feelings.* When you are alone and upset, you can take out a pencil and paper and start writing. Keep a journal. For some people, this is a great outlet.

3. *Express your sad feelings.* If you feel sad, it's OK to cry. For example, you may have been raised with the idea that showing the emotion of sadness was bad. Consequently you learned to stuff negative feelings inside. Now is the time to give expression to those feelings.

4. *Express anger directly.* I have found that so many of my overweight clients never learned appropriate anger expression. If you are one of them, I recommend that you read *Breaking Free From Anger and Unforgiveness.* In that book there are multiple strategies to deal with anger. Anger isn't a

"bad" feeling, but it needs to be expressed appropriately. You don't want to hold in anger because it leads to feelings of depression and eating problems.

5. *Determine if there is a need behind your feeling.* You can feel something intensely because it represents an unmet need. Feelings can represent a wish to be respected, loved or accepted.

BE ASSERTIVE

One reason people overeat relates to setting boundaries and telling people *no*. Perhaps you are afraid to speak up, don't feel you have the right, need to please others, want to be loved for what you do or think you have to be superwoman and do it all! Time to turn in your cape! Learn to say *no* and not feel guilty.

Saying *no* requires assertiveness. Assertiveness is behavior that falls somewhere in the middle of giving in and aggressiveness. It is not giving in to the wants of others or keeping silent and expecting people to read your mind. It is also not yelling at people and demanding your way. Being assertive is a practiced skill that helps you manage stress. Contrary to popular thought, you don't have to be angry to be assertive. In fact, I prefer you stay calm.

There are two parts involved in being assertive: 1) Know what you want, and 2) say it. One of the reasons people don't practice being assertive is because they don't know what they want. Because of this, others can manipulate them to do things that are uncomfortable. This results in feeling resentful, which leads to overeating.

Or you may feel guilty and don't believe you have the right to speak up. You do because you are someone important. You are also responsible for managing stress that comes your way. When you can do something about stress, take the initiative—speak up! Know what you want and take a reasonable position. Do

When you address problems as they occur, you won't build up anger and hold on to things that can turn into resentment.

not feel guilty about setting limits. Reduce stress by taking control where and when you can. When you do, the urge to overeat will lessen.

Speak up and let your voice be heard. When you address problems as they occur, you won't build up anger and hold on to things that can turn into resentment. Oftentimes, this is the root of overeating. Many of my female patients have to be taught how to be assertive because it is a skill they never learned. It is also something that has to be practiced.

Next time you feel the urge to overeat or binge because you failed to be assertive, practice this skill. It will get easier the more you do it. The end result will be a happier you!

Break Free From a Negative Self-Image

Overeating is usually tied to poor self-esteem and image. Hatred of your body, feeling unworthy of love and needing approval from others are common themes with people who binge or compulsively eat.

I recommend you read *Breaking Free From a Negative Self-Image*.[1] In that book, you will learn how to correct your self-image. In addition, you will learn to find your identity in Christ and not from any other source.

You were created in God's image and are not a mistake. He gave you your body, and you need to take care of it. Loathing and hating it will take you nowhere but into depression. There needs to be a basic acceptance of who you are and an effort to take care of what has been entrusted you. A healthy balance between body obsession and hatred is what is desired because the extremes create problems. Eating healthy, exercising and taking care of the "temple" are important.

Like any addiction, compulsive overeating and bingeing destroy what God has created, and they keep you in bondage. In order to break free of the hatred you feel toward the extra weight and out-of-control feelings, build a firm foundation in Christ. Know who you are, what you reflect (the image of God) and how God wants to use you. Knowing these things will center you as you grow to a healthier you.

Most of my overweight clients only look at themselves from the neck up. They avoid full-length mirrors like the plague. Doing

God loves you unconditionally. He doesn't judge you by what you weigh.

this keeps you in denial of what the bingeing and compulsive overeating do to your body. Take courage, and look fully at your body. Then realize your body image is probably distorted. When you lose weight, you hardly notice. When you gain a few pounds, you feel heavy and depressed.

God loves you unconditionally. He doesn't judge you by what you weigh. He wants to set you free from the compulsion and failure you feel, but He doesn't judge your outward appearance. He looks at your heart. As you work on gaining control over the compulsion, focus more on your spiritual identity. This is of eternal value.

STRATEGIES TO BREAK FREE: BEHAVIORAL CHANGES

Making small but important changes in your behavior will go a long way to maintaining control over food and developing healthy habits.

BREAKING FREE

MENTAL HEALTH FACT

Nutritional Changes You Can Make

1. Don't skip meals.

2. Don't go more than five and one-half hours between meals without a snack. It's a setup for a binge or overeating.

3. Eat meals and snacks in one place, preferably at the kitchen table. Break the habit of eating food on the run. You will eat less when you have a specific place to eat.

4. Eat slowly, chew your food and give it time to reach your stomach.

5. Have a healthy, low-cal snack ready and handy.

6. Eat fruit instead of drinking fruit juice.

7. Eat without distractions—turn off the TV; don't read. Be relaxed and take your time.

8. Use smaller plates to make food portions look bigger.

9. Your mother was right—eat more veggies!

10. Stick with one helping.

11. Make the kitchen off limits except at mealtime. It's too easy to wander in and open cupboards looking for food.

12. Double your fiber intake and cut your fat in half.

13. Decrease use of sugar, caffeine, salt and alcohol.

14. Put leftover food in foil or containers that are not see-through. Store them out of sight or freeze them.

15. Don't buy food that is easy to overeat or a binge food. If you

must leave your house to purchase binge items, you'll have time to think and hopefully stop yourself.

16. Grocery shop when you aren't hungry. Go with a list, and stick to it.

17. Don't go on fad diets.

18. Reward yourself with something other than food.

19. Weigh no more than once a week.

20. Exercise—make it a lifestyle as discussed above.

LEARN TO RELAX WITHOUT FOOD

Deep muscle relaxation

If eating is a way to calm down or soothe you, learn other relaxation methods and substitute those for eating. One of those methods is deep muscle relaxation. It is based on the idea that tensing a muscle and then releasing it produces a state of relaxation. So if you consider the muscle groups in your body and practice tensing all of them, one at a time, then release the tension, you should feel quite relaxed. You don't have to tense so hard that you hurt yourself! Just clench, tighten, stop the tension and concentrate on the next fifteen seconds of relaxation.

Practice this technique of tensing and relaxing the muscles. You can feel tension in your body and learn to cue your body to relax. It takes just a few minutes each day. This exercise will teach you to feel the difference between tension and relaxation.

Here's what you do. Find a comfortable and quiet place to practice. Start with a muscle and tense it. Wait a few seconds (study the tension), release it and feel the relaxation (about fifteen seconds). Repeat this with various muscle groups, including your stomach, head (eyes, mouth, jaw), triceps, back, biceps—all parts of your body, making sure no tension creeps in when you practice. Concentrate on each muscle and clear your head of other thoughts.

You should practice for about twenty minutes a day. It usually takes about twenty to thirty minutes to go through all the muscle groups and become completely relaxed. I like to have people practice when the alarm goes off in the morning and right before bed at night. This way, you start your day calm and end it the same. Practicing at night helps you fall asleep. You also learn to relax your physical body without using food to cope.

Take a deep breath

Relaxation comes in many forms. Sometimes it has to be learned and practiced. For example, if you grew up in a home with an alcoholic or abusive parent, you may not even realize that your body has carried physical tension for years. Your response to the tension may be overeating or bingeing. Alcoholic/abusive parents can create uptight kids. Kids never know when the alcoholic/abuser will be available, angry, critical, physical, kind or calm. This unpredictable pattern leaves a child tense—always waiting for the proverbial shoe to drop. Tension becomes a learned state of living. Many adult children of alcoholics need to teach their bodies how to relax.

Let's begin with an easy way to learn to relax. Before you begin, try to rate the level of tension in your body from zero (no tension—you are probably dead) to one hundred (this much tension will kill you).

Take deep breaths. When you are tense, breathing often becomes short and rapid. It tends to originate in the chest. Some people even hyperventilate, which can lead to panic. Breathing should come from the abdomen, not the chest. If you are unsure, place your hand on your abdomen, take a breath and see if your hand moves. If you don't feel an in-and-out motion, chances are you are breathing from your chest and throat.

When you concentrate on taking deep, slow breaths, you supply more oxygen to the brain and muscle system. You stimulate the parasympathetic nervous system, which calms you. Taking deep breaths can help you clear your mind. Try to concentrate on your body. Try to inhale slowly through the nose and let the air go down low. Pause and slowly exhale through your nose or mouth.

Do this over and over, about ten times. When you practice deep breathing three or four times a day, you will catch yourself breathing incorrectly and teach your body to relax. The good thing about this form of relaxation is that it is free, easy to do and can be done anywhere. You can be in the middle of a crowd, start feeling tense and take a number of deep slow breaths to calm down. Or you can be alone in the house and practice.

After you have practiced this exercise a few times, rate the level of tension in your body again on that 0–100 scale. The number should be lower. If not, you need more practice. The more often you sense stress in your body, the more you can apply this technique. So next time you feel tension creeping into your body, take a deep breath and relax! Don't eat. Relax.

The eating substitution list

Develop a list of behaviors you can do when you feel the urge to overeat. In other words, what behavior would you substitute for overeating or bingeing? Write these items on a piece of paper now because when you are fighting the urge to overeat or binge, it's hard to think of an alternative behavior. Therefore, make your list in advance. You should include behaviors you can do at home, at the office, in crowds or when alone. Think of a variety of behaviors to use, and tailor your list to things you know will work for you.

Then keep your list with you. When you feel the urge to overeat or binge, pull it out and force yourself to choose an alternative behavior to eating. For example, Mary is driving home from work and sees the 7-Eleven (a trigger for her to binge). Mary thinks about it and knows she isn't hungry, but she begins to obsess on the binge food inside the 7-Eleven (those Grandma's cookies). She remembers her list. One alternative behavior is to put on her CD and sing loudly, thus distracting herself from the thoughts of the 7-Eleven. (She puts on a worship CD and prays as well.) She passes the 7-Eleven!

COGNITIVE HELP

Self-instruction

Here's another helping tool used to control the compulsive feeling. It's designed to develop self-control.

1. Remind yourself of the problem—"I want to overeat or binge. This will defeat my progress."

2. Think about your choices—"I could binge, or I could distract myself away from food."

3. Think about the consequences of your choice—"Eating equals short-term gain, long-term disappointment."

4. Choose a different response—"I'm going to take a deep breath and relax or choose from my list of twenty items."

5. Pat yourself on the back—"I did it. I didn't binge. Good job."

If you gave in to the urge, say, "OK, I gave in. Next time, I'll slow down and think. I can do this. So I slipped up. Next time is a new opportunity for success."

Relationship issues

So much of overeating has to do with interpersonal issues. Relationship difficulties can prompt those urges to overeat. Perhaps you grew up in a home where emotional expression of feelings was not allowed and people acted out of control. You learned by watching. If family members denied or numbed feelings or coped by abusing someone or a substance, you've learned similar patterns and are now using food in unhealthy ways.

Unlearning these coping patterns takes intention and effort. You can respond differently; you aren't a victim of your past. You can't change other people, but you can change your reaction to them. And certainly you can change your behavior by refusing to use food as a cover-up or emotional crutch.

If you are in a destructive or unhealthy relationship, change how you react to the person. Changing your response changes the relationship dynamics. The other person will try very hard to get you to go back to the old way of behaving because familiar behavior is comfortable behavior, even when it is unhealthy. This is why you need support when you make changes.

Interestingly, many spouses of over-eaters say they want their partners to stop bingeing and lose weight. However, when they do, they feel threatened. As a result, spouses can sabotage weight-loss

Hanging on to anger and unfor-giveness can result in overeating behavior.

efforts. Unless you address your fears and your spouse's fears about change, change will be more difficult.

The same can be true when living in a family system. Weight loss may threaten family loyalty if all the members are over-weight. Expressing feelings directly instead of through overeating may raise tension in a family. Assertiveness skills can make people feel uneasy and unsure how to react. When you make changes, they affect all the people around you. If you sense a lack of support, you may consider family therapy or couples' counseling. Both are helpful in assisting your path to freedom.

In many cases, it is necessary to let go of

past hurts. Hanging on to anger and unforgiveness can result in overeating behavior. Read *Breaking Free From Anger and Unforgiveness* if you need more guidance in this area.[2] Forgive those who have hurt you or let you down. Then ask for forgiveness from those you have hurt.

The point is that overeating is an old friend who serves a purpose in your life. Whether it is to protect you from emotional or relationship pain, anesthetize you or keep you from looking more inward, giving up this friend won't be easy. Let me encourage you, though, there is a friend who sticks closer than a brother. He will never leave or forsake you, and He won't bring you pain and shame. His name is Jesus.

Support

Support groups can be helpful when trying to break free from any problem behavior. There is something powerful about sharing your struggles with those who can relate to your pain. And those on the same path to healing can encourage you when discouragement hits. We all need encouragement and support.

You may want to join a support group like Overeaters Anonymous. Or perhaps your church or community runs a similar type of group.

Another approach is to find one or two people who will hold you accountable for your thoughts, behaviors, relationships and spiritual walk. Don't be afraid to ask for help. We are supposed to encourage one another.

BREAKING FREE
PRAYER FOR YOU

Lord, it feels overwhelming, but help me take one step at a time. There is much to do, but I can be successful if I move in Your power. There are so many other things I can do when I hurt. I want to learn to do those things that will help me, not hurt me. There is a way out of this food bondage, and I thank You for that.

BREAKING FREE SUMMARY

Watch and pray so that you will not fall into temptation. The spirit is willing, but the body is weak.

—MATTHEW 26:41

*H*ere is a brief summary of the steps to break free from compulsive overeating and bingeing:

1. Recognize the signs of compulsive overeating and bingeing, and admit you have a problem.

2. Have your physician give you a complete physical examination in order to rule out any medical causes of overweight.

3. Start addressing the root emotional issues involved in overeating. You eat out of

emotional emptiness and to numb pain.

4. Distinguish between physiological and emotional hunger.

5. Identify triggers (situations and emotions) for overeating and chart them to see patterns.

6. Keep a food journal.

7. Set realistic short-term goals.

8. Identify your feelings, and learn to be assertive.

9. Change a negative self-image into a positive God image.

10. Give up the idea of dieting and shortcuts to weight loss. Exercise and commit to a healthy lifestyle.

11. Learn to relax without using food.

12. Make an eating substitution list, and use it the next time you are tempted to overeat.

13. Pray for self-control. With the Holy Spirit in you, you have the power to overcome.

14. Face your relationship problems, and resolve them as best possible.

15. Get needed support to make these difficult changes.

B R E A K I N G F R E E
P R A Y E R F O R Y O U

Lord, by the power of Your Holy Spirit, I will overcome this eating problem and be free from emotional bondage. Thank You for doing the work in me. As I grow in You, I will have less need to use food to satisfy. You will be my source of satisfaction.

THE HOPE

No temptation has seized you except what is common to man. And God is faithful; he will not let you be tempted beyond what you can bear. But when you are tempted, he will also provide a way out so that you can stand up under it.

—1 CORINTHIANS 10:13

A major hurdle for most people trying to break free from compulsive overeating and bingeing is discouragement. Freedom isn't usually instantaneous and requires perseverance and commitment in order to change destructive habits. Freedom is possible, but many give up because failure is such a familiar road.

The temptation to gratify your self or to use food as an emotional cover-up is intense. Usually compulsive overeating has been practiced for a number of years, but finding a way out of the grip of food addiction is possible.

I want to encourage you to stay in the fight, not because you want to be thin and glamorous, but because you don't want to be brought under the power of anything other than the Holy Spirit. Food should not rule your life. When it does, you are in bondage, and Jesus came to set you free. He wants you free. You will continue to fail in your own power if you don't incorporate a vibrant relationship with Christ into the healing process.

The trustworthiness of God is real. The joy a relationship with Him brings will turn those feelings of despair into hope.

Be ready to tackle the issues behind compulsive and binge eating. Yes, food is being abused and used for destructive purposes, but the emotional hunger that drives that compulsion must be fed. There is no program, spa, weight-loss method or exercise plan great enough to fill that void.

The emotional emptiness you feel can only be filled by the love of God. As you press into a deeper relationship with Him and learn to lean on Him, you'll lose that compulsion that seems to drive you.

People may have let you down. Perhaps you were abused, the child of an alcoholic, neglected or even abandoned. The unconditional acceptance you never felt can be realized with God. It's already done. He loves you just as you are, overweight or not. His love is not dependent on how you look or what you do. He just loves you and can be trusted.

If you are leery of trusting God because others in your life have let you down or failed you in this area, give God a try. He is like no other. He will never leave, abandon or disappoint you. The trustworthiness of God is real. And the joy a relationship with Him brings will turn those feelings of despair into hope.

Replace your desire for food with an insatiable desire for God. Be a glutton for Him. Praise and worship Him. It's the one area of life you can't overindulge! Ask the

Holy Spirit for the power and strength to overcome the temptation to overeat. It's not by might or by power, but by His Spirit. Be strong in the Lord. Avoid fleshly indulgence (overeating), and don't give in to it. As you devote yourself to living in the power of the Holy Spirit, you will develop self-control (a fruit of the Spirit). Then, be persistent and finish the race. (See 2 Timothy 4:7.)

God wants to develop self-discipline in you. It is essential to your spiritual and emotional growth. But in order to become more disciplined, you have to practice that discipline until it becomes habit. Most people aren't self-disciplined by nature.

Self-discipline is more than will power. It involves *Holy Spirit power*. Recognize your weakness, but depend on the Holy Spirit to enable you. Make the choice to grow in God and experience all He has for you. Enter into His presence and receive His power, the power to overcome.

BREAKING FREE

PRAYER FOR YOU

Lord, I praise You for always providing a way out and the power to overcome temptation. You are great and greatly to be praised.

A BENEDICTION FOR YOU

Now to Him who is able to keep you
   from stumbling,
And to present you faultless
Before the presence of His glory with
   exceeding joy...

—JUDE 24, NKJV

Introduction

1. Statistics related to overweight and obesity retrieved on line August 8, 2002 from www.cellulite.net/Obstats2.htm.

2. Rebecca Moran, "Evaluation and treatment of childhood obesity," *American Family Physician* (February 15, 1999): Retrieved online July 30, 2002 from www.findarticles.com/cf_dls/m3225/1999 _Feb_1/54113331/print.jhtml.

Chapter 1

1. Tori DeAngelis, "Binge-eating disorder: What's the best treatment?" *Monitor on Psychology,* Vol. 22, No. 3 (March 2002): Retrieved online August 2, 2002 from www.apa.org/monitor/mar02/binge.html.

2. "Eating disorders," in *Diagnostic and Statistical Manual of Mental Disorders,* 4th ed., American Psychiatric Association, Washington, DC.

3. "Obesity and being overweight," *WebMD Health.* Retrieved online February 28, 2001 from http://mywebmd.com/content/article.

4. K. Zerbe, *The Body Betrayed* (Carlsbad, CA: Gurze Books, 1995).

5. Kelly D. Brownell, "Definition and classification of obesity," *Eating Disorders and Obesity,* Brownell and Fairburn, eds. (New York: The Guilford Press, 1995).

6. The National Heart, Lung, and Blood Institute of the National Institutes of Health. Press release: First Federal Obesity Clinical Guidelines released, June 17, 1998. Retrieved online from www.nih.gov/news/pr/jun98/nhlbi-17.htm.

7. Ibid.

CHAPTER 2

1. Adapted from Linda S. Mintle, Ph.D., *Getting Unstuck* (Lake Mary, FL: Charisma House, 1999).

2. "Hormone discovery may boost weight loss," *The Virginia-Pilot* (August 8, 2002): 1.

3. T. A. Wadden, "Very-lo-calorie diets: Appraisal and recommendations," *Eating Disorders and Obesity,* 484–489.

4. Ibid.

5. Ibid.

6. J. G. Kral, "Surgical interventions for obesity," *Eating Disorders and Obesity,* 510–515.

7. A. Stunkard et al., "Psychological and social aspects of surgical treatment of obesity,"

American Journal of Psychiatry 143, no. 4 (1986): 417–429.

8. T. Loewig et al., "Gastric banding for morbid obesity," *International Journal of Obesity* 17 (1993): 453–457.

CHAPTER 4

1. Moran, "Evaluation and treatment of childhood obesity," *American Family Physician*.

CHAPTER 5

1. Linda Mintle, Ph.D., *Breaking Free From a Negative Self-Image* (Lake Mary, FL: Charisma House, 2002).

2. Linda Mintle, Ph.D., *Breaking Free From Anger and Unforgiveness* (Lake Mary, FL: Charisma House, 2002).